Wi-Fi;
How To Boost Wi-Fi Speed, DIY Hacks To Increase Wi-Fi Signals, How To Boost Wi-Fi Speed, Increasing Internet Router Speed, Solving Broadband Problems
by Martin Laurence

Table of Contents

1. Introduction

People often think slow Wi-Fi is a minefield of problems to try to figure out and will cost a fortune to put right. Where do you start? What do you look for? Well firstly it's not as difficult as you think. The reasons for slow broadband can range from your wireless hardware, an old PC, your house architecture, your Router, and even your phone line. All these things can have a huge impact on your Internet speed.

In this book I will cover a range of quick and easy methods to solve extensive problems that you can do yourself. I will provide you with simple DIY tricks to more advanced solutions to increase your speed which will in turn get you to somewhere around the full potential of your Wi-Fi.

I've been a telecommunications engineer since 1995 working for a family business and we have had a range of various telephone issues to solve in business premises and also in the home. We have networked over 300 data points for some company's right down to a single data point for senior citizen who wanted their router moved upstairs. And everything in between from people operating from fly leads to switches to showcase work in data centres.

You get a sense of what to look for and how to solve a problem thoroughly and quickly. When we were working in house premises we sometimes discovered the customer has spent thousands of pounds/dollars on buying new equipment to get round their slow broadband which had made absolutely no difference at all. It was then usually something like the incoming phone line being the cause of the problem. So from the get-go this book can potentially save you a lot of wasted money and time running around when I can tell you how to look for the problems.

I've also written a number of other books on telecommunications and specifically cabling hard-wired networks rather than using Wi-Fi which is much faster. However I wanted to also write a book that was specifically for Wi-Fi since in some cases hard-wiring isn't a feasible plan.

Broadband and Wi-Fi problems can stare us in the face, but sometimes we need an engineer to say 'have you checked this?' and that is what this book is - a helpful guide to solve your Wi-Fi issues.

Before we even get into the rest of the book - let's check our Broadband speed right now. With everything as it is with whatever you're using. You can go onto websites like 'Speed Checker' and it will tell you your maximum upload and download speed. Simply type 'Speed Checker' into Google and you'll get plenty of options. One of the top ones will do fine. Once you click onto the website and 'test' you'll be given an 'Upload' and 'Download' speed. Write these down.

This is a barometer for us to know where we stand right now and gives us a point of reference to improve upon.

So you've written both numbers down? Okay done that? We now have our current speed - now let's improve it!

Let's take a look at how we can boost your Wi-Fi.

2. Line Quality

Before we look at the Router, DIY hacks or whether our neighbours maybe unwittingly using our Wi-Fi, we need to start with the line. The analogue side of the Broadband is an indication of your phone line health - is it working perfectly? Any issues at all with line quality will affect your Broadband speed. No matter how good the rest of the network and equipment is - a problem with your line will bring everything down.

Check the Line:

Firstly does your line work? Sounds a stupid question right, but I know many people who don't use the voice side of their Broadband anymore because they have a mobile phone and only use the Internet side of the line. So this means the speech side is never used and they have no idea whether it's good or not. I've had more than couple of instances on house jobs where the Broadband side of the line works to an extent but the speech side is completely dead. This is because the data side can at a push work on one leg - one wire - albeit badly while the voice side needs both wires - two legs - to work properly. So test the line with a normal phone that you know works - make sure you have a ADSL filter plugged in to the socket too. Simply pick up the handset and you should have dial tone.

Line Quality

Secondly make calls out and ask someone to dial in and call you. Can you hear them clearly? Is there any crackling noises or breaking up on the line? We want to test that the line is clean and clear, by that I mean we don't want to hear any funny noises at all when listening to dial tone. We want a nice crisp dial tone. If you can hear any crackling, or the line cutting out then you have an issue - progress below.

Poor Quality?

If you can hear a crackling noise - unplug everything else from the network - Smart TV, other phones, and including Router. We want to eliminate your equipment as a possible problem. Take your phone to the first line box - the main telephone socket that comes into the house. Don't forget a filter too and try again. If the line is clear then one of your pieces of equipment is faulty and could be slowing down your Broadband. So you will have to plug each of your pieces of equipment one at time and keep checking the phone line. You should be able to eliminate the problem by doing this. I once had an automated home oil control unit causing a problem. This records your house oil level and automatically calls a company to deliver more when levels are low. But it had gone faulty and once removed bought speed levels back to normal . So check the line again - if it's all good then you're good to move on otherwise:

Still have a problem?

So with everything unplugged and you're still having a line problem then you have a faulty line and you need to contact your line provider. When you call up to say you have a fault, say you have unplugged everything - this is usually the first thing they ask! They will blame you or your provider if they are separate and will usually threaten you with a charge if it's not them. So just be thorough with your test. Their standard procedure is to blame you and threaten you...can't beat customer service!

Once your line is fine and/or repaired we can move on.

3. Testing Optimal Speed Test

So we have checked our line and it's working perfectly fine. Great! So onto testing the top speed of our Broadband now.

We have already tested the current speed right at the start of the book. Now we want to test the optimal speed. To do this we take our computer/laptop (ideally) to the first line box again where we tested the line quality. Plug the Router back in and switch it on. Now we want to plug a patch lead into the Router and into your computer/laptop. This is so we have a direct hard-wired link to the Router creating minimal lose of signal.

The Broadband will take about 5 minutes to see the Router so wait for all the lights to come back on and power up your computer while you wait.

Once you can see the Broadband is back on and your computer can see it, log on to the Broadband Speed Checker again and start it off. Ideally we want these figures to be faster than before. They should be a lot faster since you're plugging directly into the Router. Write down the upload and download speed.

This should be faster, a lot faster than your previous speed. So now we have established that is your fastest current speed - we have eliminated walls etc What we want to do is to get the Wi-Fi heading towards this faster speed.

4. Use the Latest Router

One of the easiest ways to make sure your network is as fast and reliable as possible is to use up-to-date hardware. My Router was a year and a half old and seemed to be getting slower and slower and I eventually changed it. The difference was night and day. A new Router will have improved firmware, more advanced aerial and the Wi-Fi signal will be superior.

Have a look at your Router unit to see how old it is. If your Router is 'Wireless A, B, and G'. These models are now considered old and slow.

So it is probably worth upgrading. What you should look for is Wireless N and the newer ones are Wireless AC. These Routers will give you the fastest speeds all round. Also look at the age of your computers/laptops. How old are they? Are they struggling with simple tasks? If so then perhaps they need upgrading.

Also if you're computer savvy then you could have a look at the network card inside your PC as it may be limited to 10/100 speeds. Desktop PC's can easily add a PCI Gigabit Ethernet network card for less than £30/$20. A notebook or all-in-one gear can't easily be changed.

Note that you'll need both a wireless N router and a wireless N card in your computer if you want the full speed boost so it's worth looking at what you currently have.

5. Changing Wi-Fi Channels and Avoiding Interference

Microwaves, and many cordless phones operate in and around the same frequency range as some Wi-Fi channels. This can cause interference and a slowdown.

So the easiest solutions to do straight away is to:

- Move the Router to a new room (if this is an option) and test the speed
- Change your phones to cordless phones labelled as DECT 6.0 which operates in the range around 1.9 GHz.
- Microwaves tend to interfere more with channel 11 so make sure you avoid any channels near that.
- Buying a dual band router can help with interference

Changing to a Different Wi-Fi Channel

Many Wi-Fi Routers default to the same channel which is 6 and when you're in close proximity to your neighbours who are using Wi-Fi too then both your Routers could be having a fight. This battle can cause so much interference that you'll all suffer from slow Wi-Fi speeds.

By manually switching to less crowded channels or one not currently used by any other networks could drastically improve your speed. The trick is to identify which channels are most crowded and which are free. Here's how to swap your router to a different channel.

- You can use software such as the free inSSIDer utility for Windows which locates nearby Wi-Fi networks and discover which channel they're on. There are also apps to check your Wi-Fi for example the free Wi-Fi Analyzer app. Start by ensuring your tablet is connected to your Wi-Fi network and then open the app and it will take you through the steps.

For inSSIDer then you do:

- Install the program on a laptop: http://www.inssider.com/downloads/

- Choose your wireless adapter. It'll immediately detect and display your network and more importantly any others nearby. The great thing is you can walk around your network area and inSSIDer will show you how your wireless strength varies in different places. Then you either move your PC's to areas with stronger signals or move the Router to a new area. But it's a useful tool for you to see faster and more reliable connections.

- Once into the program you'll see a graph that shows the different Wi-Fi networks nearby as well in different colours and the channels they are currently using along with the strength of signal.

- If you have a Laptop/PC etc. which is suffering from poor Wi-Fi speeds, then install inSSIDer there, and again it'll display your signal strength at the location. You can then try some of the other tricks in this book to increase that signal strength. You might then try a new location for your router - but be careful you don't improve the performance of this PC at the expense of the others.

- All these tests will give you an idea of whether your network has a strong or weak signal and whether the channel your Router is currently set to is too is crowded. You can then pick a channel as far away from your neighbours' as possible. It's worth noting that out of 13 channels, all but 1, 6 and 11 overlap.

- To change a channel you need to access your router's web interface. This can be done by opening a web browser and navigating to the router's IP address. The Router URL will either be printed in your router's documentation or sometimes on the bottom of the device itself. If not then simply open a Command Prompt in Windows and type 'ipconfig' without the quotes and look for the default gateway address. This is your router's IP address, and will be similar to 192.168.1.1.

- Next you'll be asked to enter the routers name and password. Again these details will either be printed on the router itself or in its manual.

You should certainly change the password to prevent anyone else accessing the settings.

- From the web page that is displayed, look for the Wi-Fi settings and the channel number should be selectable via a drop-down menu. The location of the option will differ depending on the router manufacturer. For example if you used a D-Link router - the channel settings can be found by clicking 'Advanced' from the main page. You can then select Wireless setup from the options on the let-hand menu - then chose Manual Wireless Network Setup. Make sure you save the settings and remember your router may reboot to apply the change.

There we have it, have a go and see how you do. InSSIDer is great for at least seeing what your Wi-Fi signal is like even if you don't want to start reprogramming your Router.

6. Is Someone Using My Wi-Fi?

Someone else maybe using your Wi-Fi without your knowledge. Perhaps even without their knowledge! A great many people just log onto to a Wi-Fi source and off they go. They probably don't even know if they're on their own network unless they have created their own password. Even then someone could use your network by hacking your password. The first instance is more common than people hacking.

The very first order of the day is that you change your login password and make your network private. This will make people accidentally using it impossible.

Your router's administrative console can help you find out more about your wireless network activity and change your security settings. To log into the console, go to your router's IP address.

- This can be done by opening a web browser and navigating to the router's IP address. The Router URL will either be printed in your router's documentation or sometimes on the bottom of the device itself. If not then simply open a Command Prompt in Windows and type 'ipconfig' without the quotes and look for the default gateway address. This is your router's IP address, and will be similar to 192.168.1.1.

- Next you'll be asked to enter the routers name and password. Again these details will either be printed on the router itself or in its manual.

On a Mac - Open the Network Preference - and grab the IP address listed next to 'Router'. Using your Routers IP address input this into a Internet page to bring up the Routers login page. Then you can go to:

- Connected Devices/Attached Devices/My Network/Device List

This should provide a list of IP addresses, MAC addresses, and device names (if detectable) that you can check against. Compare the connected devices to your equipment to find any unwanted users.

Bear in mind that many devices connect to your Wi-Fi these days. The list will contain laptops, smartphones, tablets, smart TVs, set-top boxes, game consoles, Wi-Fi printers, and more.

Using a WPA password is absolutely essential. A website like http://www.dd-wrt.com/site/index can among other things really help with beefing up security to a high level.

7. Find the Optimal Location for Your Router

Your house architecture can slow down your router depending on thick walls, multiple floors and how far away the router is from where you're actually using it. For example if your Router is situated at the front of the house and you're using your laptop/tablet etc at the rear of the house, you will end up with a very weak signal to access. There will be multiple walls to get through before it finally gets to you tablet etc.

So where should you situate the Router? The best position that I've found is as high up as possible, and as central as possible. So for example in the attic. The signal can rain down upon the house innards. Chances are you may have power plugs up there but probably won't have your line.

So you can either uses Router boasters or move your Router. Router boasters which I talk about later won't make the Wi-Fi faster, moving the Router is always much more effective if possible. You will first need to parallel a new Telephone socket from your Broadband telephone socket. This uses hard-wire telephone cable, run around the house to the new position.

This is actually quiet an in depth subject and can be a little tricky but I make is very easy as possible and go into detail in how to move the Router in another book I've written:

Broadband Speed: How To Increase Internet Speed, Solving Broadband Speed Problems, Internet Router Connections

I go tell you into what equipment you'll need, how to look for the easiest cable routes, and all the connection details including lots of pictures. It's an easy 'how to'. Initially you could try buying a long extension lead and extending the router out into the house to see how your Wi-Fi is affected. If your phone and tablet signals improve then your house is holding back your speed and the Router needs to be moved.

8. DIY Hack To Increase Your Wi-Fi Range

There are a number of quick DIY tricks that could increase your speed and this is probably one of the simplest. This obviously isn't the most effective method, but it's been known to add a slight improvement which could make a difference.

This is called the 'Windsurfer Tin Foil Sail'. Essentially you are creating a curved shape, like half a baked bean can, a reflective surface that you place behind your Router which will rebound the Wi-Fi signal back into the areas of the house you want it.

If your Router has antennas then you could actually create something to sit over them and hold the 'sails' in place. Then angle the homemade windsurfer into the rest of the house. I've had some success with this and it can increase the range just enough to make a speed difference. This is probably one of the cheapest and easiest tricks to try first.

You can also use an old beer can, take care not to cut yourself and slice the can in half. Then bend it so it's like a half open curved shape and placed behind the Router. It's certainly worth making a note of the speed before and after and you can gauge if this has made a difference. Other things to use could be an old cooking strainer, even curved cardboard with tinfoil attached will work.

The results won't necessarily be ground breaking but they should improve it slightly with minimal effort.

9. Boost Your Router's Signal with a Bit of Hacking

Another great way to extend your range is to hack your router by using the DD-WRT firmware which I have previously mentioned.

Here is website and it will guide you to which one to install:
http://www.dd-wrt.com/site/index

By installing this you will not only get a slew of great security features but it gives you the option to boost your transmitting power. You can actually program your Router to give a higher output. Almost like fitting a supercharger to a car engine. Most Routers can handle an increase up to 70 mW without causing any issues. This should give you increased range. However this can be dangerous for your Router and damage it, so before doing this be sure to look at your Routers documentation to see if it can handle this increase.

You can find tutorials for installing the firmware on the website. Simply go to the router database, and enter your router model. If the router is known a list with matching entries is then displayed indicating if the router is supported and if an activation is required. For personal use one activation is for free whereas multiple for a company for example is charged.

If your Router can't be found then go to the Router Detection page, a page will give multiple options to potentially make your Router work and will require you finding out what chipsets your Router has. This can be complex for someone who isn't too tech savvy.

10. Boost the Wi-Fi Signal with Repeaters and Old Routers

Another easy option is to extend your Wi-Fi range. Wi-Fi extenders piggyback on your existing Wi-Fi connection and rebroadcast to get a greater range of signal.

I've compiled a list of various models which have been given positive feedback from a number of sources. As you can imagine these will constantly change and upgrade as of Feb 2016:

1. Netgear EX6200
2. Asus RP-N53
3. D-Link DAP-1320
4. BT Dual-Band Wi-Fi Extender 600
5. Linksys RE6500
6. Zyxel WRE2205

They won't reach as far as wired connections and they won't improve your overall network speed but they will get your signal to another floor for example. Generally they're cheaper and less hassle than any alternative.

Turn Your Old Router Into a Wi-Fi Repeater

If you happen to still have your old Router then you can also turn that into a repeater and boast your signal. You will need the DD-WRT firmware again to turn the old Router into a Wi-Fi repeater.

Here is the link to the Repeater information which will guide you through the process. Although this won't allow you to increase speeds over Wi-Fi, it will allow you to transmit the Wi-Fi signal throughout the home.

11. Reboot Your Router on a Schedule

If you're one of the many folks that has to reboot their router every so often so it doesn't lock up or drop out then there is a solution. Firstly the best solution is to simply buy a new Router because this could be hiding other issues. If you're pretty sure it just needs powering up and down to get it back on track every so often then we have 2 solutions.

1. You can buy a time clock that plugs in and you can set it to power up and down at a specific time. So once every two days, once a week.
2. You can once again use that wonderful firmware DD-WRT which as you now know now is full of useful features.

http://www.dd-wrt.com/site/index

It's also worth checking your router is not running hot as sometimes they keep locking up because of overheating. Place your hand on the unit and feel it. It should be cool to touch. It's worth raising it up using wooden blocks so the air can get all around it.

12. Final Testing

Once you have made a few of these changes then retest your broadband speed. Conduct the test exactly as you did the first time around so that both tests are identical. You should have a speed that is faster than your initial speed test and be something heading towards your absolute fastest when you plugged your computer directly into your Router. Also remember time of the day may affect the test, school time when kids get back seems to really drag down the speed around me. However your general speed should be much better.

So we have reached the end of my guide on how to boast your Wi-Fi and hopefully cure some of your Broadband speed problems along the way. I hope the information I have provided will be of use to you and given you a head start on maxing out your Broadband speed.

Remember to consider safety first when using any tools and ladders and ask for help when going up a ladder.

I have a number of other books I've written all linked to data networking and telecommunications in particular about data networking your house, moving your Router and moving a telephone socket. If you are still suffering poor Wi-Fi and you think your house architecture is a problem then hard-wiring is far superior and worth considering as the next level up of problem solving.

Finally please leave a review of my ebook - I would be most grateful!

Thanks and all the very best!

--Martin

Get All The Books In The Series:
- <u>Broadband Speed: How To Increase Internet Speed, Solving Broadband Speed Problems, Internet Router Connections</u>
- <u>How to Install a Data Network in your House</u>
- <u>How to move a Telephone Socket in your Home</u>
- <u>How to Install a Data Network in your Office</u>
- <u>How to make Money from Data Network Installations</u>

www.ingramcontent.com/pod-product-compliance
Lightning Source LLC
Chambersburg PA
CBHW071835200526
45169CB00018B/1530